IN CULTURE WE TRUST

www.CreativeFederation.com

Content

Turn your culture into value.

"Logic will lead you from point A to point B. Imagination will take you everywhere."

-Albert Einstein

Your outstanding and unique culture is worth to be reflected in your revenue. The values you are possessing can be transformed into consulting, coaching, or professional services. This book will help you to overcome one of the biggest obstacles to achieve this. It will turn your passive wisdom into active wealth, help for others and a bigger cultural contribution.

Being a cultivated person you and I sense that we can help and contribute in a much bigger way. There are people out there right now that would profit from your help and you can profit from helping them. You can use the strategies of this book to transform your possible prospects into consulting clients that will pay you monthly for your knowledge or services.

This book will show you how you can make people eager to become your client. It is possible to put you in a position in which you can pick and choose your clients. The methods introduced in this book, you can implement directly without any former selling knowledge. It will show you ways how you can get your knowledge in front of the right people who will appreciate your support. You will find out how easy it is to use the new possibilities to get connected with your right community. Stop trying to work with everybody to scrap a leaving. With the knowledge of this book, you will know how to choose wisely the people you are working with and supporting. The methods are specially designed for people who don't like to be pushy. Instead, you can stay in a cultivated interaction zone. It will show you how to eliminate resistance from possible clients and put you instantly in a position of authority. Even should you not decide to take someone is a client you will be able to generate goodwill for the future and have them talk positively about you. As an alternative to putting you into a complex business and tech structure, you are going a cultivated way. This approach is specially made for people who want to stay focused on their cultural competence. If you are able to use Facebook you are good to go. Even if you prefer simple tools like a piece of paper, a pencil, a calculator and writing letters you can start immediately. You are free to modify the methods, according to your needs. At its core, this method is showing you the essence of a prospect to client transformation. Instead of waiting for the right opportunities or door to door network begging, you can start even when you're brand new and nobody's ever heard of you. You will prove yourself through your uniqueness and value instead of fame, hype or credentials. With the knowledge of this book, you will gain a complete blueprint of the most powerful sales methodology without becoming a salesperson. No sales pressure, convincing or traditional "selling" will be necessary for you to convinced high ticket clients. It is specifically designed for cultural people Who Hate "Selling". Instead of manipulating people into a say this method cares about influencing and guiding prospects to their best possible outcome. By using your natural intuition for helping others you will become a trusted adviser and get rewarded in the process. The methods will show you how to develop profitable long-term relations with your clients instead of quick sale mentality. It is the intention of this book to show you How To Make More Sales, without convincing anyone of anything. The system of this book has been proven over and over in the cultural world and my career.

Let's have a closer look what we will cover in our lessons. In this course, we will talk about the outstanding possibilities that you have, with the opportunities that are opening up.

Right now there's a change going on from which you can profit. You will find out how to transmit your values and your wisdom to the right people so you're profiting from it. Your uniqueness and your competence can be an inspiration to others and you can bring value to others, and the best thing is this course will show you how to profit from this process. You will learn how easy it is to influence others, but it doesn't stop there. It is about a profitable partnership. This course will show you a process, how to make the right choices for the people who are benefiting the most from you and who you are profiting from. You will find an easy procedure how you can transform those prospects into your clients so you can achieve together much more.

OCCAS
Your Possibilities

"The future belongs to those who see possibilities before they become obvious."

- John Sculley

But now let us first talk about "your possibilities". One of the most important takeaways in cultural consulting is that quality matters more than quantity. Often when you are starting something new, we want to get connected and we want to work with everybody and this is the wrong approach.

We should start to work from the beginning with the right people. It is wise to pick and choose from the beginning because in the end you are getting paid for bringing the most value to someone so the decision who we are working with can be really easy, who will benefit the most and in the fastest way from working with us? There are certain clients who will gain a lot of value from us so they will be no resistance to share value with us. In other words, if we are able to find a person who we are helping to get the bigger fish, it will be not a problem to get some slices. It is worth to put some effort to find this group of people for whom you able to get the better and quicker results. When for those clients;

Results Equals Value,

it will be really easy to keep them happy and you will really have a stress free work. Seeing it from this perspective, let us begin to think how we can achieve such clients. Let us keep in mind only model build around our core competency is able to bring the value to other people. Since the laws of business and marketing are not really working in the cultural world, we will build a consulting model that is easy to operate and easy to maintain for you. The longer you are able to stay with your core competence, the more value you are producing and the value equals the gain you are getting from the clients.

SIGNIA
Your Value

"Try not to become a man of success, but rather try to become a man of value."

-Albert Einstein

Remember, it's not about quantity, it's about quality. The benefit of such a construct that is built around a value has the benefit that you don't have to make lots of sales. If you are delivering the necessary value, it's not a problem to get enough reward monthly from few clients. See your payment from their perspective of value. If your client is able to harvest a lot of more value through your help, it is not a problem to hand you down a fraction of this value as your payment down. Also from the other perspective, when the client is getting more value through you, he will also be willing to stay for a longer time with you.

The best thing is that with time these long-time clients are referring you so no extra marketing and no new selling of your service is needed because valuable clients will be your best marketing you can get. This approach is a completely different way of thinking because it depends on the longtime agreement of value. Since this model is completely different in its core philosophy, you would have no luck with the usual approach of hard marketing, selling and pushing the client. This is in high ticket consulting and coaching an advantage. Most of the consultants moving into the cultural market are still using the old significance model. They are trying to get new clients attention through showing off how impressive and great they are. They are hoping if they impress enough people, all others will believe them and we'll figure out what they could do for them.

They are hoping for the reaction of the network as an echo chamber. Some networks are working like this; they are getting the attention to the wrong kind of people in the hope for more projects or corporations later on. Most of such hype is ending at the point where real clients want some value. Such a system is not built around the one thing that matter, the value your client will receive in the end. In the beginning perhaps to see you a core competence from the perspective of your significance can be really hard. But remember we are dealing with delicate culture. You can really fast feel with the old approach like a pompous car salesman. This never works. Trying to pose an artificial significance is not building an accommodating situation. In this way, you're not supporting the development of your core competence or real value for your clients. Client value matters. No matter how glamorous you are and no matter how the network is celebrating you, the customer counts. He will only care about the values he can get through you for himself. The selfishness of the client is a great thing. It is taking the pressure from you to be something you are not. You can only concentrate on your core competence and what value your client can get in the end.

The only thing that matters is helping the client. To get new clients is really easy when you only care about one question; How can I help my clients to get the values he or she is desiring through my core competence? If he's convinced that he will get his values in the end, there is not a problem of getting a portion, a fragment of those big win as your payment. In this way, any marketing is really easy. It's all about convincing someone that you can get him to value he or she is desiring trough you. Advertising is becomes really easy – it is just about the value of the client.

Shifting the client acquisition from you and your personality to the values for the client is making a lot of things easier. You are remaining just with your core competence and solving problems for people. If it works out, this person becomes your client. Getting clients is becoming a game of confidence. Your core competence is giving you the confidence to solve problems. On the other hand, a solved problem is giving your client that confidence in you. Since your possible client's expertise and knowledge is smaller than yours, it's really easy to convince them. All we have to solve is a fraction of his bigger problem. If this fraction is bothering him the most and it's holding in the most back from getting any value, he will be easy to convince. If you can solve this bottleneck problem for the client, he's experiencing the value he's getting from you and begins to hope for new value in the future. No selling, no clever marketing is necessary - results are evidence. All you have to do is to be in a position where the client wants you to help him even more in the future. It is logical for him to use us as a tool to get to his values in a more efficient way.

BENETIC
Your Benefit

"Strong people don't put others down... They lift them up."

— Michael P. Watson

Let us talk in this chapter is about your benefits. We will have a look how the new opportunities, the new path are generating growth for you and are benefiting your development. In the last chapter, we have seen that we can take completely new perspective to see our client. Now, let us take this perspective and turn it into a mechanic that will be a great advantage for you. As we have seen, high ticket clients care only about solutions and results. If they have the confidence in you getting them results, they don't care about your network, about your pedigree or about your reputation.

This new approach has also a great advantage for you. In the old approach, you had to divide your energy. On the one hand, you had to spend a lot of energy and resources in building up your reputation and your network, and on the other hand, you also had to prove your core competence in bringing results. This new approach is client-centric, so all you care about are results for the clients and the confidence you had to build up. It is almost an open secret that in the cultural world, in reality, no one likes show offs. Show-masters like Dali was are the exceptions and they are not the kind of people who are making the real money in art and culture. It might be that they are getting the attention, but in the end, the clients are deciding for the people who are getting the job done. So if you're someone that likes to talk about culture, instead of just bragging about yourself, this approach is just right.

High paying clients made already a lot of experience, so bragging wouldn't work with them. That's why the new concept is making it so easy to get new clients because we are demonstrating that we can help them by actually helping them. The high ticket client is focused on the results and the values for him. In this approach you have already solved a problem for him, even when it is a fraction of his or hers bigger problem, you are now in a situation that is different.

You have turned the tables around; the client had experience that expansion of the value through you can be fulfilled. So he or she more likely wants the rest of the job also be done from this moment on through you. "Never change a working system" is still a good wisdom for many. Clients like to invest in you when it already worked out for them.

In this way no clever marketing is necessary, no pushing from your side. All we have to develop is a situation in which it is easy for the client to pursue us. In this situation, results and values are more important than any network, hype or any pedigree, all you have to care now is a situation in which the client could get you in a way which will increase his confidence. The easiest way to raise the confidence is a process of qualification, but this time the other way around. To get clients wanting you instead of the other way around builds a stronger confidence and bondage. Once someone is choosing something, he or she will go a long way to stay consistent with his or her decision. From this perspective, that new approach of getting clients becomes a really easy process for you. At first all we have to get the attention of the right clients. Since we are living in the age of new media and the social media, this will be easy, so our message is getting only to the right kind of people. Our core competence is making us understand the "bottleneck problems" of our right client. We don't want the attention of everybody.

You just want the attention of the right client, in the right situation, looking for the right solution from us. If you see your expertise from the perspective of a novice there are numerous situations which are straightforward for us but for a beginner are solution magic. Remember, the client is just interested in the result and the benefit. The help and the solution we are designing should be centered around the client. When we are designing the solution, we should just focus on the client and the way he is seeing his problem. This is not the moment to show off all our possibilities or what we could do for any kind of possible client. We are only getting his attention when we are understanding and solving a problem that he has now from his perspective. Keep in mind; this process is not about getting random clients, so we have to be selective at this stage. We only want the client for which the solution of the bottleneck problem is an indicator for your ability of solving later on his big problem. The free solution we are bringing is just a milestone to greater value, not the end result. To minimize the risk for the client and to build up goodwill and confidence from the beginning, this bottleneck solution should be free. In this way you are building a untroubled crossing to use your pay service later on.

Contact you client in the right way. You should know your client so you know which media is the most convenient way for him to get the information about his solution. This part of the process is all about getting together a list of possible right clients. If the right person is reacting to your free solution you have a contact to follow up. If you are working with the old media like advertising magazines, you are also good to go. You are ending up with a whole address list of the people you have sent the free solution perhaps as a booklet. If this is to much work there is a easy way. You can also use the more convenient way of the new media. Especially through social media you can advertise so people are coming to your website. If they leave an email address, they're getting that booklet as a free PDF. Even though this process right now is not lucrative, remember we are after high paying clients. So only one client will get you all the money back that you have invested in this "marketing". Keep in mind; the numbers of prospects don't have to be big. We are addressing a very specific problem from a very specific client with the claim that we can help.

The process doesn't stop with the first free solution. We can follow up. Since you know the bigger real problem of your client, you exactly know where your client is after you have solved his first milestone of a bigger problem. Most likely we know how long it takes to solve the bottleneck problem. If we are now following up with a question;

How it has worked....

We are showing that we care. We also can start a process that will transform him or her into our client. In this set up you can't lose. Even when it's not have worked out, you have built goodwill. You have established that you have concerns about their goals. Also when it's not working out for them you are gathering information how to make your free giveaway even better. The follow up is not the moment to push the prospect into becoming a client. It's worth to be patient as you know; we are in the world of the high ticket clients, waiting pays off.

For many prospects the free solution will work. Already now we have shown that we can get results, we built a desire for more and we have proven ourselves as a possibility to get more value. Now we want to develop a bond that will convince the prospect into becoming a client - and in the end to invest a lot of money in us. We are using the momentum of the result experience in a way, so the prospect is qualifying to us. We want to get him or her, the feeling that we are the right match. A simple verification process is a strategy to increase the prospect's confidence. From his or hers perspective, it is important to enhance the feeling of being in good hands and minimizing risk. Achieving this is the perfect position to turn a prospect into a client. Instead of pushing him or her to become our client, we will develop a different scenario.

It is possible to turn the situation around. A situation in which he is asking us to do the job for him and becoming a client is just a conclusion that the client wants. To achieve this, all we have to do is to use the old wisdom that people are supporting what they are creating. As an alternative of just pushing our solution and our plan to progress, we will cooperate together. It is about giving him the feeling that he's developing together with us a plan how he can solve his challenges. It is hard to repel what the client himself has co-created. To achieve this, we will guide the client with questions. Those questions are influencing him or her to develop a plan in his mind. The plan he is arranging has to be a solution for his situation. About this arrangement, you are certain, that it will bring him the right solution and the values he desiring. If the prospect has the feeling of developing something on his own, he will be more convinced that it can work out. The confidence in getting more value has risen in your prospect. This is the time to reinforce it with an inspiring cultivated conversation.

In this talk until now your prospect has the feeling of developing the ideas and their plan on his own, so he's more convinced of it. Since an own plan seems achievable, his desire to get it done to get the values will increase also. To keep the prospect visualizing progress with the plan is main focus of your guidance in conversation. To keeping up the desire for solution is important. A point has to be reached in which the prospect is convinced of his "own ideas" and all we have to do, is just to ask; if this seems to be a good plan for him or her. Remember: people are supporting what they are creating, this will be our first YES because our prospect has the feeling of having an own plan. Don't worry about being cut out of the process from here. Nevertheless, the prospect is still not having the competence to achieve the solution. To put it in a simpler example: the prospect is convinced with the plan that it takes a car to get to the finish line but he does not have a driving license. The prospect has an overview of the plan but is not knowing how to execute the details. From here you can get the second YES - that will turn this prospect into a client. The prospect desires solution with the developed plan, not the execution of details he is not confident about.

In the prospect mind the achieved value matters most. You have proven your ability so you are the logical choice. It is logical because we put effort into the selection of possible clients. We have picked a prospect from which we know that we have the core competence to achieve his values. Knowing that we are in a more efficient and convenient for him it's easy to make up his mind. It's more logical for him to say YES. We didn't pick the one that has a potential competence of doing it on their own. Sometimes it can be helpful to remind the client of the details. Underline how long it took to achieve your status of expertise that is necessary to execute the particulars. Most prospects imminently understand that they are paying years of study, try and error and frustration with your fee. Client should be focussed on the big peace they are getting, not the small slices from the top for you.

All it takes are guiding questions that are leading to logical conclusions. As you can see this process is really very cultivated. Even when a prospect is saying NO, there's always a reason that will help both parties. The confidence that you have built in the client and the goodwill that you have built up will pay off in the future. The knowledge that you have gathered in the process will also turn out priceless. This kind of starting point for getting clients is really outstanding. It is beginning with understanding, care, confidence and a good starting plan. Let´s get more into the details of the process in the next chapter.

CONTRAL
Reaching out

"Networking is never easier than when people are coming to you. "

-Tahl Raz

In this chapter let us find out how you can reach out with your values to contact the right kind of prospect. Let us talk about opportunities, how you can transmit your wisdom to the right people so you are gaining them as an audience. Many people that are working in the cultural field are misunderstanding the signs of time. For many participants in the artistic world, it seems that the world is stuck in old fashion, tradition and the old ways. In a way, this is great news for you because a part of our competition is also thinking this way. Of course, when you started 40 years ago, it made sense that all your possible clients were living within a radius of 100 kilometers to reach them.

As you remember, our perfect client is solution and value-oriented and we will use the new opportunities to get in front of our perfect audience. You have the outstanding opportunity that right now the new media has already become part of our culture. It is not only convenient and efficient but also already a proven tool. In business and consulting, especially three ways of getting your message in front of the right audience has proven to be working. In this book, we will concentrate on those three. LinkedIn is a great tool to reach out if your client is a kind of expert. With Facebook, you can reach nearly everyone, even if this person is on Facebook in disguise. Should you perfect client turned out to be really conservative then perhaps direct mail is still the best solution for you.

Let me start perhaps with the most efficient and easiest one, Facebook. Perhaps at first glance, Facebook seems to be trivial. But the mechanics behind Facebook are just outstanding to reach every person you can just imagine. Facebook has built an incredible database that is cross-matching all the data you can think of. Even when your perfect client opened a Facebook account under a fake name, it is possible to get his data through cross-matching. Your message will end up in front of the person you have decided for by setting criteria. Does your perfect client depend on criteria like the demographics, level of wealth or special interests? It's not a problem to reach them. With over 500 categories and growing, you can be very precise who you want to reach. Just imagine for a moment you have a high priced consulting. It would be really a waste of your resources to contact not the right people. It is a waste of time, effort, and money to put your message in front of people who perhaps are interested in your help, but are not able to pay you in the end. If you get the message in front of a person with the right criteria's you can win effortlessly. Parameters like certain threshold of income and interest, for example in antiquity are helping your message to get through. In the end, your communication will make more sense for the right person. You can narrow down the criteria until you core competence is targeting the right client. In this way, the first solution that you offer is absolutely matching the prospect that received your message. In the same way, you can reach out through LinkedIn and through direct mail. When you are using traditional media do some research first. Investigation about the kind of medium, like a magazine that your perfect customer reading when he's opened for your solution, is gold. When you build your business around getting the value to the client, you have a good understanding of all aspects of her or him. Reaching out becomes a game of quality, not quantity. In this way, you don't need so many prospects as you might think. Putting money in high quality targeted advertisement pays off.

Let start to understand you as main content of your advertisement. You can become the inspiration for others that you can use to gain prospects. Let us find out how your performance, your values can convince others. As you have seen it is today a great opportunity to get your message in front of the right prospects. In this chapter, we will have a look, how do we transform the ones that are getting our message, into prospects that will get involved with us. This will be really easy because we are gaining their trust by actually demonstrating that we can help them. By just putting out "your message", you are already on the winning side. If your perfect prospect is reading your message and you're showing that you understand his situation. In this way, you show that you care. This alone is creating a feeling of a bond. Your follow up process should increase this feeling in every step. The simplest solution to achieve this is by formulating what the prospect is troubled by into a precise question. As an expert, you understand the bigger problem. But you also understand the symptoms. These troubles are showing up in your prospects troubled mind everyday life. Address them in your advertising and become a path to solution.

You can develop a story that will guide the prospects and bring them clarity. In the most cases, the prospects troubled mind is not clear and confused with different aspects. If the prospect will just read the solution, he will be still troubled if this is the right solution for him. But when a prospect is reading a question involving the solution, he is getting awareness that is drawing all his attention. If you have found the most logical question your prospects should ask himself you are getting into his or her head. Your question and story can give him the feeling that he is not alown. When you can just offer a free first solution, you get your prospect involved with you in most cases. You can also expend this process with a second approach. You can even instantly increase the bonding with you possible client. For this approach, you really need expertise in your core competency. The knowledge about the values you client will receive in the end and understanding about his troubled mind. This knowhow you are using to predict the path you client will go through to achieve his desired values.

With such a process we can - not only deliver the information in every stage that is needed, but we are aware of the "feeling" the prospect has in every stage of his path to direct him better. Let's say, for example, our core competence is about counseling people how to build up and lucrative art collection. For us as experts the solution is pretty easy - Invest in art at the right time, increase value, and then sell at the right time. Form our perfect clients perspective the situation is absolutely different. He is involved and often overwhelmed in everyday work and most likely don´t even see the necessary stages. To make things simpler, let's pick an example and say it our perfect prospect is an art lover with money to invest. So how do we reach out to such client?

On social media, we have already decided for the right criteria like high income and following or buying magazines about art houses like Christie's or Sotheby. This will be our prospects characteristics. Just to message them to sell or buy art would not help us to get involved and to build a bond with them. Since they are at the beginning of the investment, most likely they will be overwhelmed and confused about all the possibilities to invest money. Of course, they would react to a message with a question what is to invest in, but even better is a question that would involve they're feeling right now. We are addressing the confusion, our message could be:

Five questions you should ask yourself to get rid of the investment confusion.

Those questions are perhaps some tips they are getting for free after opting into our website. In return, we are gaining so much more. We have their address and the opportunity to message them, to contact them directly. Now this prospect has won some confidence in us because we brought the first solution. They know how to get rid of investment confusion. The best thing now for us in our follow up, we can get even more involved with them. The prospect will be really happy if you show that we care and ask how the questions have worked out and since we are now knowing exactly at which point the prospect is, we can help him even more. In this case, the next step is to choose an investment form, so now the feeling is uncertainty. Keep in mind. If we have chosen something that is actually helping them and is giving them already the feeling of value, we are on the winning side. There will be a certain point in which the prospect will just ask us for more help. You surely remember our formula;

a new client is someone problem solved through your core competence and the outlook for more value.

At this stage, we have just generated a perfect prospect. Now it's time to turn this prospect into a client. As you will see, it is not difficult.

RASPIRE
Your Influence

"One of the best ways to influence people is to make them feel important."

— Roy T. Bennett

In this chapter, let us talk about how you can influence your prospect. Let us find out how you can support your prospect in the best possible way, but in a manner that also will have value for you. In the chapters before we have prepared our prospect in the best possible way. Now let's have a closer look to all the steps so you have the feeling of guiding your prospect to becoming your client. As you remember we have offered our prospects free help and he already experienced our value. In our follow up, we have explained and pointed to the benefits and the value he has received. This is also the perfect time to explain why we are helping him or her because right now the prospect is asking him or herself why you are helping him for free. Not answering this question in advance would diminish the confidence the prospect has already built up. If this question remains open, the prospect will remain skeptic about us. If we are up front open about what our agenda is we are gaining trust. It is much easier, later on, to turn the prospect into a client. In this situation of trust, it's much easier to develop a risk-free situation and offer for the client to which he can't say NO, and will ask us in the end for our help. To increase your confidence, let us have a closer look at each step on this path.

To gain trust on the first step, we have offered our prospect free help. We have shown in this step not only that we understand the prospect needs, but also understand his feelings. Already here we have the possibility to put in a small offer; it can be by helping them to work out some smaller details. This is just a small hint but is enough to show the prospect that some value will follow in the future. In the next step, it's really important to make the prospect understand that value, the possibilities and the opportunities you are creating through your support. It's not about boasting about yourself. It's about showing which benefits are leading to which value through the service you are able to provide. In this way, the client is able to compare the huge value he's getting through you to the fraction of your fee. This is also the best moment to explain why we are doing this. To avoid any scepticism, just formulate what your advantage would be is not enough. It is transparent, but it would be not helpful because it is about you. Remember, it's all about the client and the values he is wanting.

Turn the perspective from you to the prospects gain. Your profit is just a by-product of this value. It is a side advantage that you are able to get, by helping him or her. To make a simple example: it's like telling the prospect that you want to help him to catch the big fish because you just need the head for a trophy or the skin for fish oil. Focus the prospect on his gain and your payment as the smaller compensation of getting him there. You should know and understand your perfect client well. In this way, you know how to put things into perspective. You know also when it's not a problem to get a fracture of his achieved value. You are able to get him. Nevertheless, perhaps the prospect has right now the feeling that someone is just trying to sell them something. We want to eliminate this fear upfront in the next step.

This can be really easily achieved. Remember, it's all about the confidence of the prospect that you can get him the values he desires. The easiest step to achieve this is to prove that you have the confidence to get these values. Your trust in your own core competence should be high. You should be so certain that you are offering your first help for free. You can go even further; free the prospect from any first disadvantage. . When the customer has the feeling you have wasted his or her time, you are even paying them a certain amount of wasted time back. From the perspective of the client, you must be really confident in your abilities if you can lay a wager on the outcome.

Sounds crazy but something like this is increasing the confidence. The client feels secure because you're putting yourself out there. You are taking the risk for him or her. Remember right now, you're not taking any risk because right now you have not taken him or her as a client. As you can see, the last step has reversed the situation. Now the client has nothing to lose, gain everything and believes that you have to lose a lot.

This is also reversing who wants whom. From the perspective of the prospect, he believes having both advantages on his side. He has the outlook to get his desired values at our risk. This is psychological reverse position. It has the advantage that the prospect fears now to lose a risk-free gain. You are gaining now trust, showing confidence and gaining a cultivated sales free position. It is putting you in a place of authority. In this situation you have a reason to explaining why we are not taking on everyone. The prospect can hope now to be picked. You are in control and the clients have to have certain qualities and for filling certain criteria's. Of course, since we have already used this qualities and criteria for our search most likely the prospect you are in the process has those qualities. Because you are putting yourself at possible risk there is an understanding and hardly someone will feel repelled by you and run away. If someone does, we're getting rid of the time wasters.

That last step of qualification is not here to look down on your client. It is all about increasing his confidence with a verification process. Now you have the advantage of questioning your prospect and you are really getting the data you are needing to make the decision. If you really can help your client, you are not putting yourself at risk. On the other hand, the prospect has from the beginning the feeling that everything that is happening is just about him and this qualification process is making everything tailor-made for him. If this process is happening in a cultivated way, not only the position has reversed, but also the confidence trust has increased. With this positioning, it will be really easy to transform the prospect into a client.

ELECTILE
Your Choice

ELECTILE

"It is our choices... that show what we truly are, far more than our abilities. "

-J. K. Rowling

This chapter will help you to make the right choice for your clients. Let's find out how you can pick the right prospects so both of you are getting value out of your cooperation. Just imagine for a moment. In which position has the process brought you so far. You are able to attract the right kind of prospect. You are building a lot of goodwill in a cultivated way and you are now the position to choose between the best prospects. The best fit will become your clients. Since you have put yourself at risk to work for free or even to repay the client for wasting his time changes the game. From now on it's really worth to put some effort in the process of turning him or her into a client. Remember this is culture we never want push ourselves on someone.

So how do we get the prospect to ask us or obviously conclude to become your client? The easiest way to achieve this is to work backward from the values you will be achieving for your client. There will be a position or a situation in which your client has what he or she wanted. This is the endpoint, but most likely to get there, there are some points some milestones privies to achieve. One of the first conversations is about walking the client through every milestone so the outlook at the goal seems achievable. Most likely you already have the qualification data of your prospect, know his goal and his problems, so you have an idea or vague plan how to get him there. Break the plan into milestones so the prospect is not overwhelmed by the conversation. Every milestone and every position your client has to go through has some very important factors that are involved. Some of those are known to you as an expert. But some of them have to be added from the knowledge of your client. There is an easy procedure for getting the client into naming his or her problems or "symptoms". Ask targeted influential questions. He or she is coming up with the challenges and also solutions by digging deeper with questions. The questions are less about the challenges your prospect believes to be important, but the one you know as a expert are significant. All you have to do is going through your list the factors or challenges you know that will contribute to the success. For example: You prospect may believe that the color of the dress is important during an exhibition, but you know that the matter of advertisement is more significant to success. So you guide and dig deeper to clarify the challenges of high class advertisement. You can transform them into qualities and characteristic that sound less pushy. In this way, you can involve them in a cultivated conversation that is constructive and not indiscreet.

Let's have a look at the example of building a lucrative art collection again. The highest value you are bringing to your client is the profit from his art collection. In this scenario, the first thing you should know is his expectation about this profit. If you don't want to ask about the exact numbers, you can transform this factor into a comparison. You can formulate a question by comparing the profit to other forms of investment like gold or stock exchange. This question will answer the high or low expectation of the profit. Since you are the expert, you will know that certain expectation of profit can be only achieved by a certain investment. Again, since to stay in the culture zone demands being diplomatic it is worth rephrasing. Formulate it delicate just to ask about the numbers is a little bit indiscreet. Since you are the expert, you can ask if their investment is in the amount of: a Picasso, a contemporary artist or a regular art fair. This is asking about a high, middle or low profit in a diplomatic way. Letter on in the process with him as a client you can get concrete. This question should be put together not too vague, but in a way so that the prospect has the feeling that something tailor-made and discreet is in development.

If you know in advance that the project is very sophisticated it's a advantage to take care about some details in advance. Is the case is a little bit more complex; it is wise to involve such questions in the written qualification process before hand. In this way you are on the safe side; you are getting all the information you are needing even before you are talking the first time to the prospect. Since those questions are diplomatic and not indiscreet, you could put them together into a document or a PDF and send it as one of their follow-ups. To make your prospects, sending the answers to questions back in advance has a big advantage. On the one hand, you are getting rid of possible prospects that don't know what they want, remember you are at risk and must know in advance if you can help them. On the other hand, you are getting rid of all the people who are just wasting your time. You are ending up just with their prospects who could become your clients. Try to bring yourself in a position in which you have all the information you need to be really honest with your possible client about the help you can offer. If you have asked the right kind of questions, you already know how you can be of value. If you are confident about your help, you gain authority and can estimate the risk. You are taking on an investment of time to gain a big win with a long time client later on. Remember get only together with prospects for which you are ready to do the initial work for free. If this is the case it is also the best time for the first appointment. The best thing about such position of yours is that you have a good overview. You already know or can evaluate the path you will help them that is making your service necessary.

This first appointment may be informal through telephone or Skype or whatever fits your kind of clients. Remember right now you have all the information, you have figured out by now that some clients with a proven background will bring you in so much profit that it is worth the investment. Some client are even worth it to let them fly in so you will have a personal conversation. All the effort, on the selection until now, were leading to this conversation. All the previous work and preparation made it possible so you can now focus on the prospect and have a conversation in style. Put your best foot forward in a way that the prospect will enjoy himself. This conversation is to make it easy and efficient for the prospect to achieve a feeling of clarity. It can be an uplifting talk about his vision of the future values, you have the advantage that you are the one with a plan, a guide. You have a red outline of a map and influencing questions that are guiding through the conversation. But remember, it is about increasing the prospect's confidence, not a protocol. Never push the client with questions that are making it obvious that you are exceptionally crucial if they want to succeed. Especially when it is about art it is about bonding with a human being.

The red line of your plan is just a mark during the conversation. It is showing you in which stage of development you're in. When the conversation becomes distracted, you know the point you should move it to.

To make the thing effortless for you, I have prepared clear stages you can lead your prospect through. In this way, you can concentrate and focus on transforming the prospect into your client. Again, this is not a protocol you should strictly keep. You can modify the process according to your needs. First, you are not starting right away with efficient questions.

You're taking the time for human bonding, of course when a - no time no-nonsense person is in front of you can change the approach. In this part of the conversation, you underline the common values that you are sharing with your prospect. This "small talk" can end when you have the feeling that you are agreeing on a common goal, on a common value or the client is beginning to say yes more often. We will start the conversation by asking some questions about his or her goals. The answers of the prospects are very important. Take notes and underline what is an important emotional value for your prospect. When something seems to be very significant; dig deeper. They are the foundation on which later on you will, together with him or her develop a plan. As said before you are going into the conversation with knowledge and a vague plan, but to put yourself at the risk of just have developed a wrong one is unnecessary. This conversation is about letting your prospect say a transform version of your plan. Your plan modified and out of the mouth of your prospect will increase the confidence to become a remedy that you can prescribe to them. Of course, we will not force this remedy upon our prospect. We will in the next stage, check for the satisfaction because only with the agreement of the client, we can move to the last stage of accepting him as a client.

Before I introduce you to every stage of this conversation, remember to get yourself before the appointment into the right mindset. Your mindset and your intention will be the driving force of this conversation so we will really take care of it. The first thing you should remember that we are in the culture world. The common goal of you getting together with your prospect is to drive the culture forward. What counts are the cultural values of your prospect. You are here to serve and to help him to achieve those values. Of course, you are here to make business, but your profit is in direct correlation to the values you will achieve for the client. You have put a lot of effort until now to develop a situation in which the prospect has the confidence to trust, and the desire to work with you. You have even developed a situation in which that prospect has qualified to you and you have all the necessary information how to help him. Any way of being pushy selling hard or making the customer feel uncomfortable would be poison to what you have built up so far. Remember, there is nothing to fear because you are in an outstanding position. Even when nothing will work out and you are not accepting him or her as a client there will be a win to both of you. You have helped him with some clarity. He is on the path to achieving value and you have built so much goodwill that he or she will talk about you very positively as free marketing. With such a positive impact all doors will remain open for perhaps future projects.

CLIENA
Your Clients

"A life is not important except in the impact it has on other lives."

-Jackie Robinson

Now it's time to talk about your client conversation in detail. Let us find out how you can transform your prospect into your client and do it in a very cultivated, respectful way. That first stage of our conversation is all about bonding and asking questions. As said before we already right now have all necessary information about our prospect. We also know why and where he wants to go, so we should have a plan how we will get him there. But now comes the part that is really a little bit counter-intuitive.

To transform the prospect into a client what we have learned naturally or growing up is not helping. We have often been conditioned to help people, just by telling them what to do. If you would just tell your prospect how clever you are, what to do and push your plan on him, it wouldn't work. Remember:

People are supporting what they are creating.

To guide him or her to an own idea is much better. Use questions to build a bigger vision. It is giving him or her the feeling of creating a plan. Don´t let the prospect feel it is your prepared plan. You and he or she are developing ideas in a cultivated inspiring conversation. This is "magic" that is giving the prospect confidence. In this way, you will be much more successful. Our job is to know what the client wants to achieve and bring in milestone by milestone step by step closer to his goal. We are not dragging the prospect to his or her luck; it's a hike with a partner. The procedure and questions to achieve this can be really easy.

We have a lot of information from the qualification procedure of our prospect and a plan. This conversation is about connecting them to our future client as a human being. Those are high ticket clients; it matters how satisfied they feel. First, we have to ask again about the end goal, but this time in a way in which we are finding out in which way he will be satisfied with the end goal. It may be that many clients are having the same goals like profit or the next exhibition, but the feeling of satisfaction is always different. For some people, it's the feeling of security, for others it can be the feeling of pleasure and even some people want to reach their values to feel loved or being accepted. The client will only happy with reaching his or her goal when this emotional value is also reached. With questions that are digging deeper, you're helping the prospect to define his very own future vision. Be sure that the prospect is clear about his very own vision. When you are getting positive signs and the client is excited about the future you can begin to make the path to get there real. From a point when you start to talk about details it's time to pop the most influential question you will ever ask. You're asking the prospect to imagine reaching her or his very own vision in advance. You can ask; what has to happen so he will feel good about the goal? What are the factors that are necessary so the prospect is imagining himself or herself reaching his goal? How it would look like in detail?

To put this in an example: A car is something that brings us from A to B a bus is the most efficient way to achieve this. A high ticket client wants to get from A to B but hardly would he do this with a bus. The questions we are asking is about why and how he would be satisfied in achieving B and then we can help him better with the best car type to achieve this. For one client it will be a fast car to save time, for another a pompous limousine to impress. In both cases you provided the client with car and reaching point B, but the HOW does matter. Do not skip over emotional value answer. Take your time. This kind of influential questions is giving your prospect immediately satisfaction. It is picturing them seeing himself reaching his goals in his way.

During the process of developing this vision, the prospect became aware of all the factors that are necessary. We also provided guiding questions about the significant milestones. In this conversation the positive and negative factors have been collected by you. These aspects are helping or hindering him or her to achieve the goal and get the values. Now it's time to introduce slowly your necessity. If we ask now as the second question:

What needs to happen in the next 12 months (or the most likely time period) so he will be happy and feel satisfied with the results he's getting?

The prospect is most likely clear what the path to successes will include. More than likely he can come up with a list of all the things that are between now and the positive future. This question has two benefits. It will make him name all the factors that are hindering or helping him to move forward. In this way, we exactly know what will be our job. We know where we can bring our core competence in. The other benefit is. The prospect is already imagined himself or herself working together with us and achieving his desires. This presumption or mental picture will make the transformation from prospect to our client later much easier.

Let's get back to the process of our conversation. Right now we're at the point where we are transforming ideas. The vision and the factors of our possible client are becoming an achievable plan. As we remember:

A new client

=

Someone problem solve through your core competence and that outlook for more value.

What does it mean in this context? The prospect is seeing himself achieving his goals with your support. Your core competence counts. The logical conclusion for him or her would be to ask for our help. So our goal in this conversation becomes to guide our prospect to this conclusion. The fastest way is again the use of questions. They are helping to imagine an achievable plan in which our core competence becomes necessary. You have written down the factors and the milestones the prospect came up with being convinced he has to achieve. These are the one that are obvious to him or her. All you have to do now is just to underline some of them. Of course, you should pick the one that are making you service crucial. Again don't push your necessity, stay in the framework of a cultivated conversation. It is like mapping out a game field and keeping the prospect inside it without being too forceful. The focus of the prospect should still remain with the values and goals the prospect wants to achieve. On the other hand, don't let the client get too distracted with his or her own ideas. They should stay in the structure according to your preparation you have made before the conversation. It is all about making your core competence essential for the realization the clients' vision.

As important the guidance of an agreeable conversation is, keep competence in your mind. You are the expert and authority, value only useful suggestions and ideas of your prospect. They should also be the once which are fast and efficient to work through and have a significant impact on the values the prospect wants to achieve. Since you're in a conversation that should be not long and informal, you should only decide for one or three points. If you can pick the one for which you have prepared a readymade solution you are giving the prospect sovereign experience without loose ends. And again, it's not about pushing the solution onto the prospect. We are rather asking suggestive questions with a back door of just discussing possibilities. Remember avoid anything that makes him feel like you're wrong as an expert. A strong NO from your prospect would undermine the confidence you have built up so far. Your solution should be put in questions that begin like:

What are you think would happen when...

Have you ever tried to...

But don't get too vague or let the prospect just have his way. This will make you look spineless. The goal of your suggestive questions is to make your prospect, repeat your very own solution, but in his words and with the addition of the factors, he only can know. This great strategy of leading the conversation has the advantage of never being pushy. It is about generating the good feeling for your prospect of getting all the inspiring ideas on his own and becoming clear about his future. BUT in the frame of your core competence that is securing the wanted outcome in the end. Remember the example of the cars; your job is to get your future client from A to B. He or she can choose the type and color of the car, not the choice of putting the steering wheel in the luggage space.

There will be a moment when the client is echoing your plan. As soon you have heard your most important solutions out of the mouth of your prospect, it's time to move to the next stage and we will develop together with him a remedy. All we have to do is just put the solutions your prospect "came up" or have repeated in a logical order. In this way, he has agreed to the part solutions and we can put it together in an effective plan. This is not the big detailed plan; it has to provide the confidence to achieve their highest possible impact. And again, we are not putting the plan on the prospect, but we are developing together with him a path to venture together. The most efficient way to develop this path or remedy is to use the call and response method. This is easy to achieve because it is letting a lot of free room for development. All you have to do is to put:

If I understood you right X, so you will/can achieve Y

If I heard you right X so you will/can achieve Y

in front of every point of the plan. X is always your feature Y is the milestone goal of the Prospect. Let us take an example again, the art collection. The big goal is to increase the value of the collection and one of the milestones is the presence of the collection in the market. According to your expertise, it can be boosted by inviting experts and gallery owners to a private exhibition. In this way you know that through relevance, the value will be increased. Instead just pushing this solution onto our prospect, we are letting him signing with his words that this is a good idea. To make it easy for the client, make it to a series of questions. You can start with a question:

"If I understood you right;
you want to increase the value of your
collection so you can increase your profits
in long term. "

The answer would it be of course, YES. Then we are putting the next question.

"If I heard you right, you already know
some gallery owners and some experts that
can achieve a presence of art collection in
the market"

, most likely again, she or he will say, YES. So good so far, but the best thing about this method should you get a NO or not quite right, you can immediately react with another solution in asking another question. You are getting a NO for a possibility or his base data instead of a NO for your expertise. You should immediately acknowledge the new information.

"Good that it came to your mind. This is useful information, so we know we need to get in contact with more experts and galleries."

Never let the prospect feel wrong or forgetful. Formulate your solution to this NO case, as the next suggestion. The question would be

"So do you think it would be a good idea to put together a contact list of possible galleries and experts, so you can achieve a presence of the art collection in the market".

Again, we will wait for the answer. With every answer the client is signing up that this is a good idea. The last question in this series could be to use your specific knowledge. Use for example you researched of the clients background that the prospect is having a wonderful villa that will be a superb location to invite on the experts and the galleries. The question would be,

"As I have understood, you have a wonderful house in which a much more personal bond to the experts and the galleries could be developed."

Again, we give time for the answer to modify and develop the perfect remedy. This process seems to be long, but it is creating a whole series of "YES" that is making it nearly impossible to say "NO" to the whole process. Keep the length of the developing plan reasonable so it sounds never overwhelming. Better simpler, than compound; later on when he becomes your client, you will have enough paid time for complex problems. Don't worry that the prospect may just take your ideas and go. Remember, you have picked only the milestones and solutions that are making your core competence necessary. Also, the question and answers are making your prospect aware how much details and how many steps it will take to achieve the next position. So in the end when he or she really cares about their end values, he will hire you as an expert to make the path more efficient. The harvest of the call and response metal is a pretty good plan that is pre-assigned through your prospect.

All we have to do right now is to move to the last stage and just accept the prospect as a client. Most of the prospects will already during the process talk about you as someone who they are working with. If the guiding questions are chosen well, you'll just have to accept. Especially if at the beginning of the conversation, you have put a clear picture of achieving his goal by working with you together this point will be easy. Often a longer pause will make the prospect ask you to become your client so you can start with execution. Should the situation not be clear after repeating the whole plan, all you have to do is just to say,

"Yes, this is achievable, I will (first task) and let you know by (next meeting call)"

or "Yes, this is just down my street, would you like me to support you to implement the plan so you can move forward."

This question is really simple but efficient. The prospect mind is on the value he feels confident about and he pre-assigned to all the solutions. Your help is just the next logical tool for achievement. As you can see without any selling, without any pushing, you have won a client. Your starting position is really outstanding. You have been asked to or you have accepted someone as a client. In this way, you are a much stronger authority in contrast to someone that pushed a client over. You have also indoctrinated a plan that you can put to work. This plan feels natural developed to your client and will prove that you can help them by actually helping them. You are also on the safe side with future work. Remember that there are many milestones you know of as an expert, but you didn't want to overwhelm the prospect now. They shouldn't come up in the first conversation but they are your work quarry.

ELEVISION
The progress of your business

"Vision is the art of seeing what is invisible to others."

- Jonathan Swift

In the last chapter, let us talk about the progress of your business. Let us find out how you can lay the foundation for your legacy and grow together with your clients. In the chapters before you have experienced: How you can turn your culture into value just by having a cultivated conversation. It is happening without any pushing, without any hard selling.

You are able to get clients.

What is turning your prospect into your client is your core competence. In the moment of your conversation with your prospect, it was easy for him or her to develop the feeling he had all inspiring ideas and solutions. Nevertheless, this was only possible because you are the expert. You have the bigger perspective. Remember the prospect has to go through the average day journey, with all the daily confusion. For him or her, it's really difficult to keep the big picture, to have a map of the whole situation. Just to have an outside perspective can really do wonders to the cultural world and bring the clients good value. Your own expertise has often not be much bigger than the one of the client. Just by having a different perspective, you can help others and also learn from every participant in the cultural world and from every challenge. That's the advantage of being an expert, consultant or a coach; you are growing with your clients.

All you need is the willingness to help others by turning your culture into value so you are contributing to the value of someone else. In this way, you're always on the winning side. There's still another aspect of this business. Some people that are new to this kind of business have some problems to ask or get the money. They are thinking it is nevertheless, culture and culture should be free. Part of me understands this perspective. On the other hand with the years of experience, I have found out that money is an achievement tool. It is actually the value that will keep the client executing what you have prescribed to them as a remedy. Remember, you are becoming part of one of the highest paid professions. In this career, it is possible with just a small number of clients to have a prosperous life. You are also able to build an outstanding heritage. Just imagine for a moment, you are becoming part of a profession in which everything is turning out positive. Culture has an outstanding impact on our civilization. No matter if your contribution is great or small with ever client you are pushing the culture and the development forward.

Your Future

"Live the Life of Your Dreams:
Be brave enough to live the life of
your dreams according to your
vision and purpose instead of the
expectations and opinions of
others."

— Roy T. Bennett,

There is no reason for not starting. No matter what you are doing right now you will always find time to consult and help others as a side business. Even with just one client, you are putting yourself in a position in which you are developing future values. As said before: not only are you growing with your clients but your experience will bring you to the point where you can just switch full-time into your consulting. Without much effort, you are generating a monthly income from otherwise passive knowledge. Often the clients even are not needing your expertise constantly but still paying a monthly fee so they have always an expert on their hand. Instead of coming up with profitable ideas and trying to sell them, you are waiting for your clients to bring in challenges that you can work on.

Don´t let money hold you back. Stop worrying about how much you can charge. It is depending who is your client. If you stop thinking about your fee from your position you can gain more. Think of the value you are helping someone to get. In this way, you will increase your confidence in charging more. Think about it this way.

Even when you possible client is making just 135.000 a year you are prospering. This income is giving your client 11.000 a month. According to crude rule, you can always get 10% of it without much resistance. So it is not a problem to get 1.100 without bargening. It must be something that he or she values of course. You are earning 1.100 every month with one client, because you care and support cultural values someone cares about.

This is just one client, most likely he is not the only person with a similar problem. Remember the cultural market is growing right now; people are needing your help. Even when this sounds fictional to you, you can start smaller. If you are afraid of charging four digits you can decide at the beginning to set a discount. You just get rid of it after the first clients. You can put a 50% discount, in the beginning, leaving you with 550 extra a month. Remember it is all about the end value for the customer and your ability to support him. It is up to you to find out how helpful you can be. Just think it this way, you are valuable, it is just a matter of finding the person that can reflect your value in your payment. But even in the worst scenario: with making no profit, you'd have nevertheless helped someone, generated goodwill, earned experience and contributed to culture.

With culture you are working at the very core of what is perceived as value, so you are working in a field with the highest possible profit possibilities. Since in the most cases you only need just your brain and a way of communication you have low overhead and low fixed cost. No extra costs are needed for fancy client baiting and show-off or even marketing. You clients care only about their results. Most likely they will do word of mouth advertising for you. Consulting and coaching is also a possibility for you to uphold a maximum of freedom. You are deciding how many clients you are having and how much you are working. You will not be tied down with a lot of technical or bureaucratic liabilities because all you're doing is talking to people. All you have to care about are the values they are after and a cultivated dealing with them that will keep them happy and satisfied. This feeling of satisfaction will also help you to grow your business in the right direction. You can be selective about who you work with. Instead of piling the clients you only deciding for those who you are happy with and they are happy with you.

It is my personal opinion; everyone who has cultural knowledge and can help others should do so. I want to thank you for reading this book and remember, you are now qualified. There's no reason not helping others and becoming part of one of the highest paid professions with one of the highest growth rate.

www.CreativeFederation.com

www.ingramcontent.com/pod-product-compliance
Lightning Source LLC
Chambersburg PA
CBHW070317240526
45467CB00045B/524